Activities Workbook

Business Finance

Les R. Dlabay

James L. Burrow

SOUTH-WESTERN
CENGAGE Learning™

Australia • Brazil • Japan • Korea • Mexico • Singapore • Spain • United Kingdom • United States

Business Finance: Activities Workbook
Les R. Dlabay, James L. Burrow

VP/Editorial Director: Jack W. Calhoun

VP/Editor-in-Chief: Karen Schmohe

Acquisitions Editor: Eve Lewis

Sr. Developmental Editor: Enid Nagel

Editorial Assistant: Linda Watkins

Sr. Marketing Manager: Nancy Long

Marketing Coordinator: Angela Glassmeyer

Sr. Content Project Manager: Martha Conway

Manager of Technology, Editorial: Liz Prigge

Technology Project Editor: Sally Nieman

Manufacturing Coordinator: Kevin Kluck

Art Director: Tippy McIntosh

Cover Designer: Lou Ann Thesing, Thesing Design

Cover Images: © Image Bank

Printer: Globus Printing
Minster, OH

For product information and technology assistance, contact us at
Cengage Learning Customer & Sales Support, 1-800-354-9706

For permission to use material from this text or product,
submit all requests online at **cengage.com/permissions**
Further permissions questions can be emailed to
permissionrequest@cengage.com

ISBN-13: 978-0-538-44508-5

ISBN-10: 0-538-44508-4

South-Western Cengage Learning
5191 Natorp Boulevard
Mason, Ohio 45040
USA

Cengage Learning is a leading provider of customized learning solutions with office locations around the globe, including Singapore, the United Kingdom, Australia, Mexico, Brazil, and Japan. Locate your local office at: **international.cengage.com/region**

Cengage Learning products are represented in Canada by Nelson Education, Ltd.

For your course and learning solutions, visit **academic.cengage.com**

Purchase any of our products at your local college store or at our preferred online store **www.ichapters.com**

Printed in the United States of America
4 5 6 7 8 9 10 16 15 14 13 12

Contents

Name _____ Class _____ Date _____

Chapter ● 1 ● Study Guide   Financial Fundamentals

Part 1   True or False

Directions   Place a *T* for True or an *F* for False in the Answers column to show whether each of the following statements is true or false.

Answers

1. Money includes coins, paper currency, and checking accounts.

    1. _____

2. Financial activities of governments involve borrowing funds to build factories.

    2. _____

3. Increased borrowing by consumers and businesses usually results in lower interest rates.

    3. _____

4. A trade deficit involves a country importing more than it exports.

    4. _____

5. The first step in the personal financial planning process is to evaluate alternatives.

    5. _____

6. The *opportunity cost* of a decision is what a person gives up when making a choice.

    6. _____

7. A life insurance company is an example of a deposit financial institution.

    7. _____

8. Check-cashing outlets are more expensive than services at most other financial institutions.

    8. _____

9. *Capital expenditures* refer to payments for current operating expenses.

    9. _____

10. Property taxes are a major source of revenue for local governments.

    10. _____

Part 2   Multiple Choice

Directions   In the Answers column, write the letter that represents the word, or group of words, that correctly completes the statement.

Answers

11. Coins, bank notes, checks, and debit cards are commonly referred to as (a) financial instruments (b) financial services (c) money (d) liquidity.

    9. _____

12. The participant in a financial system that collects taxes is (a) consumers (b) nonprofit organizations (c) government (d) banks.

    10. _____

13. If freezing weather damages orange crops in Florida (a) interest rates will decline (b) higher consumer prices can occur (c) the money supply will decline (d) lower inflation would result.

    11. _____

14. A location where long-term debt and equity securities are sold is called (a) a risk market (b) a money market (c) a development bank (d) a capital market.

    12. _____

15. The final step of the personal financial planning process is to (a) review your progress (b) set financial goals (c) evaluate alternatives (d) create an action plan.

    13. _____

16. An example of a deposit institution would be (a) a credit union (b) an insurance company (c) an investment company (d) a check-cashing outlet.

    16. _____

17. A common use of funds for businesses is (a) revenue (b) borrowing (c) money from investors (d) capital expenditures.

    17. _____

18. Business activities within one state are referred to as (a) municipal business (b) intrastate commerce (c) interstate commerce (d) regional economic development.

    18. _____

Part 3 Matching

Directions   In the Answers column, indicate which financial system participant is best described by each statement.

A.   consumers

B.   businesses

C.   financial markets

D.   government

E.   financial institutions

F.   nonprofit organizations

Answers

19.   Refers to banks and credit unions.

20.   Locations for buying and selling stock and bonds.

21.   Collects taxes to provide public services.

22.   Provides community assistance that may not be offered by government.

23.   Often must report financial activities to stockholders.

24.   Includes households that buy goods and services.

25.   Provides loans for individuals and companies.

19._____

20._____

21._____

22._____

23._____

24._____

25._____

Part 4 Activities

26.   Five main factors affect the value of securities. For each of these items, listed below, give a brief description (in your own words), and give an example of how this item might cause the value of a stock or bond to increase (or decrease) in value.

Factors affecting security value	Description	Example
Supply and Demand		
Future cash flows		
Risk		
Liquidity		
Interest rates		

This flowchart represents the three main participants in the financial system of a country.

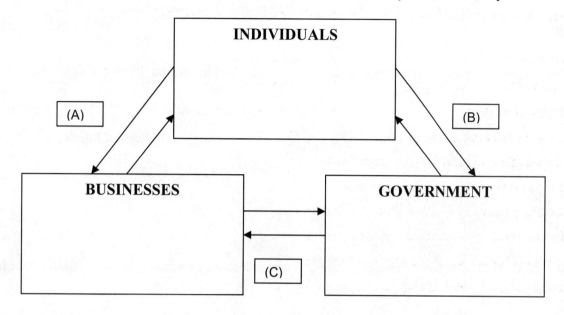

27. In each box, describe a financial action of the group participant.

28. What are various financial interactions between individuals and businesses (A)?

29. For area (B), what are some examples of financial flows between individuals and government?

30. What types of financial flows might occur between businesses and government (C)?

31. Describe difficulties that might occur among these groups when various financial flows are interrupted or stopped. What actions might be necessary?

32. Sources and Uses of Funds: Every organization requires money for day-to-day activities. The three common sources of funds are (1) revenue from sales, (2) funds from investors, and (3) borrowing. The two main categories of uses of funds are (1) current expenses and (2) capital expenditures, or long-term spending.

Select a local business or other company. List the (a) sources of funds, and (b) uses of funds that the organization might come across.

(a) Sources of Funds   **(b) Uses of Funds**

33. For each step of the personal financial planning process, describe an action you might take today or in the future.

Step 1   Determine Current Situation _____

_____

Step 2   Set Financial Goals _____

_____
(Be sure your goal is (a) realistic, (b) specific and measurable, (c) time-specific, and (d) action-based.)

Step 3   Evaluate Alternatives _____

_____

Step 4   Create an Action Plan _____

_____

Step 5   Review Your Progress _____

_____

Name _____ Class _____ Date _____

Chapter **2** Study Guide   Financial Environment of Business

Part 1   True or False

Directions   Place a *T* for True or an *F* for False in the Answers column to show whether each of the following statements is true or false.

Answers

1. Financial decisions of businesses and consumers are influenced as much by the state of the economy as by any other factors.

1. _____

2. Scarcity means deciding which wants and needs will be satisfied and which will go unsatisfied.

2. _____

3. The government has the primary influence on economic decisions in a command economy.

3. _____

4. In a market economy anyone can start and operate a business if they have the resources and ability.

4. _____

5. The two primary ways governments are involved in the organization of businesses are in legal requirements and taxation.

5. _____

6. The type of ownership structure that will have the greatest difficulty in obtaining financing is the corporation.

6. _____

7. Stock markets, bond markets, commodity markets, and currency markets are all examples of financial markets.

7. _____

8. Capital markets are used to finance short-term debt of less than a year.

8. _____

9. Most businesses operating in the U.S. today are largely unaffected by the global environment.

9. _____

10. An exchange rate is the value of one currency in terms of another.

10. _____

Part 2   Multiple Choice

Directions   In the Answers column, write the letter that represents the word, or group of words, that correctly completes the statement.

Answers

11. Which of the following is not a principle of a free enterprise economy? (a) right of private ownership (b) competition among businesses (c) a major government role in the economy (d) freedom of choice

11. _____

12. The form of financial ownership in which profits can be taxed twice is (a) sole proprietorship (b) partnership (c) corporation (d) none of the above.

12. _____

13. The length of time invested money is controlled by others is known as the (a) term (b) conditions, (c) agreement (d) return.

13. _____

14. The organized exchange of the ownership shares of public corporations is a (a) capital market (b) financial market (c) commodity market (d) stock market.

14. _____

15. A company that transcends national boundaries and is not committed to a single home country is (a) a foreign national company (b) a global business (c) an international corporation (d) a virtual business.

15. _____

16. The largest trading market in the world is the (a) U.S. stock market (b) foreign exchange market (c) long-term capital market (d) international investment market.

16. _____

Part 3 Matching

Directions In the Answers column, indicate which term is best described by each statement.

A. resources

B. demand

C. market economy

D. corporation

E. financial risk

F. money markets

Answers

17. The amount of a product or service that individuals want to buy to satisfy their wants and needs.

17._____

18. A distinct legal entity formed by completing required legal documents in a specific state.

18._____

19. The possibility that an expected profit will not be achieved.

19._____

20. The means available to develop solutions for unsatisfied wants and needs.

20._____

21. Specialize in buying and selling financial instruments for short time periods of a year or less.

21._____

22. Based on the combination of the decisions made by individual consumers and businesses.

22._____

Part 4 Activities

23. A bakery is determining consumer demand for their specialty product—decorated cakes. The chart below describes the supply and demand for cakes at various prices the bakery might charge. Using the data from the chart, write a paragraph discussing the relationship between supply and demand for the cakes. Why is it important for businesses like the bakery to have this type of information when producing or selling a product? Based on the information provided, what is the market price for the cakes and how many cakes will the bakery sell at that price?

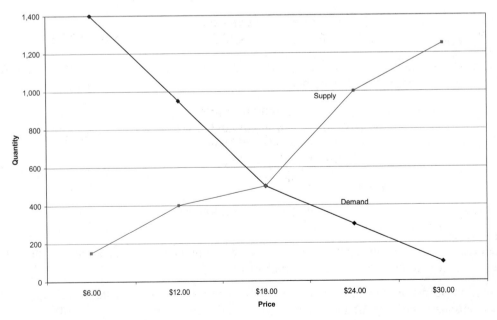

Supply and Demand for Decorated Cakes

24. There are three primary types of economies based on the way economic decisions are made in countries. Examine the three columns below. In the first column, the three types of economies are listed. In the middle column, descriptions of how economic decisions are made are provided. The last column identifies several countries. Demonstrate your understanding of the types of economies by drawing lines that connect the correct type of economy with the definition and then with the countries that have that type of economy. You may need to use the Internet to gather information about the countries in the last column. When you have completed the connections, identify two other countries that you believe fit each of the types of economies. Compare and justify your choices with other students.

Type of Economy	Description	Example Country
Traditional	What is produced and consumed is based on the combination of the decisions made by individual consumers and businesses.	Haiti
		Cuba
Command	The basic needs of individuals and families are unchanged for generations.	United States
		Rwanda
Market	Government decision-makers determine what goods and services are needed and how and when they will be produced.	China
		Japan

Additional examples of

Traditional economy _____ _____

Command economy _____ _____

Market economy _____ _____

25. In a recent year, the Internal Revenue Service reported the number of U.S. businesses filing tax returns by type of ownership structure. The table below shows the total number of sole proprietorships, partnerships, corporations, and limited liability companies and the revenues earned by type of ownership. Complete the table by calculating the total number of U.S. businesses, the total of all business revenues for the year, and the percentage of total businesses and total revenues represented by each ownership type.

Type of Ownership	Total Number	Total Revenue (in thousands)	% of Total Businesses	% of Total Revenue
Sole Proprietorships	17,904,731	$ 1,020,957,284		
Corporations	5,045,274	17,636,561,349		
Partnerships	1,338,796	1,829,568,091		
Limited Liability Companies	718,704	344,751,557		
Totals				

26. International trade requires the exchange of foreign currencies. Business people need to be aware of the currencies of trading partners and the current exchange rates of the countries' currencies. Use the world map below to complete this activity. Identify one country from each of the continents shown on the map. Write the country name on the appropriate line below. Identify the country's location by writing the appropriate number on the map. List the name of the country's currency, the current exchange rate, and the value in the country's currency of a sale of $10,500 US at that exchange rate. An example is provided.

Continent		Country	Currency/Symbol	Exchange Rate	Sale Value
North America	1.				
South America	2.				
Europe	3.				
Africa	4.				
Asia	5.				
Australia (Oceania)	6.				
(example)	x.	New Zealand	dollar NZD	1 USD/1.43481 NZD	15,065.46 NZD

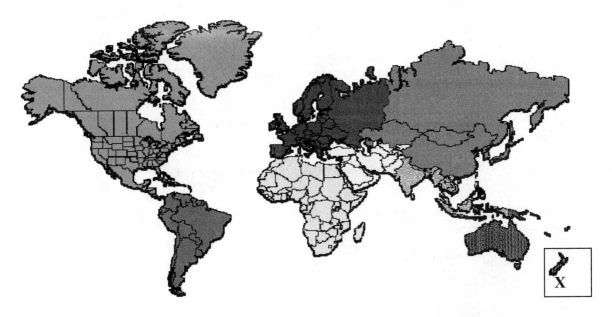

Chapter ③ Study Guide   Financial Management Planning

Part 1   Unscramble

Directions   Unscramble the following vocabulary words that were discussed in Chapter 3.

Answers

1. sesats

2. aalhetbcnees (2 words)

3. dgescipanrubteesdic (2 words)

4. piacudbtlaegt (2 words)

5. heteawcsolfmtnast (3 words)

6. locltarela

7. rtecrdio

8. dpinercaieto

9. uuavlretfeu (2 words)

10. cmtsaeeonitenmt (2 words)

11. pselartneuve (2 words)

12. tieulaemnevfomoy (4 words)

1._____

2._____

3._____

4._____

5._____

6._____

7._____

8._____

9._____

10._____

11._____

12._____

Part 2   Matching

Directions   In the Answers column, write the word or phrase from Part 1 above that correctly matches each definition below.

Answers

13. The current value of an amount of money to be received at a future date based on a specified investment rate.

14. Differences between budgeted amounts and actual financial performance.

15. An asset promised by a business to a creditor if repayment of a loan isn't completed.

16. The difference in purchasing power of an amount of money at a future date.

17. A decline in the value of an asset as it ages.

18. Shows how cash is used by a business during a specified time period.

19. Identifies the assets, liabilities, and equity of a business as of a specific date.

20. The amount to which an amount of money will grow in a defined period of time at a specified investment rate.

21. Provides a view of the financial changes in a business that have occurred during a specific period of time.

22. A plan to acquire and finance long-term assets of a business.

13._____

14._____

15._____

16._____

17._____

18._____

19._____

20._____

21._____

22._____

Part 3 Yes or No

Directions Indicate your answer to each of the following questions by placing a check mark on the line under *yes* or *no* at the right.

Yes   No

23. Is the first step in financial management for a business is to establish financial goals? _____ _____

24. Are investors in businesses typically not concerned about the rate of return they will receive? _____ _____

25. Are the four characteristics of a business goal that it should be specific, measurable, realistic, and established for an identifiable period of time? _____ _____

26. Is the basic accounting equation Assets + Liabilities = Owners Equity? _____ _____

27. Are all sources of revenue as well as all expenses of a business for a specific period of time itemized on an income statement? _____ _____

28. Does a profitable business have to worry if it experiences periods of time where there is a lack of cash? _____ _____

29. Can budgets be considered to be a roadmap for monitoring business activities and performance? _____ _____

30. Is an interest rate the cost of borrowing money expressed as a percentage of the amount borrowed? _____ _____

31. Is a greater amount earned with simple interest than with compound interest? _____ _____

32. Are investments affected by inflation as well as by interest rates? _____ _____

Part 4 Activities

33. Read the following information about a business loan and use it to answer the questions that follow.

The Barnard Corp. needs to build an expansion to its current production facility. It approaches the First National Bank and is granted a 15-year loan for $985,000 at a rate of 8 percent per year with the interest due paid at the end of each year. To secure the loan, the First National Bank asks to hold the title for the administrative office building of the Barnard Corp.

1. Who is the creditor? _____

2. How much is the principal? _____

3. What is the interest rate on the loan? _____

4. What is the amount of interest the Barnard Corp. will owe for the first year? _____

5. Who is the borrower? _____

6. What is the collateral? _____

7. Is the interest simple interest or compound interest? _____

8. In what section of the Barnard Corp.'s balance sheet would the loan be listed? _____

9 In what section of the First National Bank's balance sheet would the loan be listed? _____

10. If the Barnard Corp. paid only interest at the end of each year and then paid off the loan at the end of the loan's term, what would be the total amount paid by the company? _____

_____

10

34. Use the following information and prepare a balance sheet for the Hadkins Company in the space provided.

Date: July 31, 2---. ***Current Assets*** Cash $72,800 Accounts Receivable $125,220 Inventory $69,900 Prepaid Expenses 15,300 Operating Supplies 142,850 ***Long-Term Assets*** Investments $325,000 Vehicles $83,950 Land $186,400 Buildings $437,000 Capital Equipment $194,500 Accumulated Depreciation $59,950 ***Current Liabilities*** Leases Payable $27,045 Loans Payable $85,590 Accounts Payable $77,100 Taxes Payable $39,050 ***Long-Term Liabilities*** Mortgages $398,200 Pensions Payable $430,000 ***Owner's Equity*** Stock $407,825 Capital Surplus $75,000 Retained Earnings $53,160

The Hadkins Company
Balance Sheet

July 31, 2xxx

Assets	**Liabilities and Owners' Equity**
Current Assets	***Current Liabilities***
Cash	Leases Payable
Accounts Receivable	Loans Payable
Inventory	Accounts Payable
Prepaid Expenses	Taxes Payable
Operating Supplies	***Long-Term Liabilities***
Long-Term Assets	Mortgage
Investments	Pensions Payable
Vehicles	**Total Liabilities**
Land	
Buildings	**Owner's Equity**
Capital Equipment	Stock
Less: Accumulated	
Depreciation	Capital Surplus
	Retained Earnings
	Total Liabilities and Owner's
Total Assets	**Equity**

---

35. The following table presents six months of cash receipts and cash payments for Ranchoe Restaurant. The business' beginning cash balance is $8,490. In the graph space below, draw one line representing Ranchoe Restaurant's cash receipts for the six months, another line for the monthly cash payments, and a third line representing the monthly cash balance. Then record the end-of-month cash balance for each month on the lines below the graph.

	January	February	March	April	May	June
Cash Receipts	$29,563	$30,888	$24,123	$27,050	$33,998	$28,005
Cash Payments	$31,556	$24,801	$27,850	$32,990	$31,000	$30,125

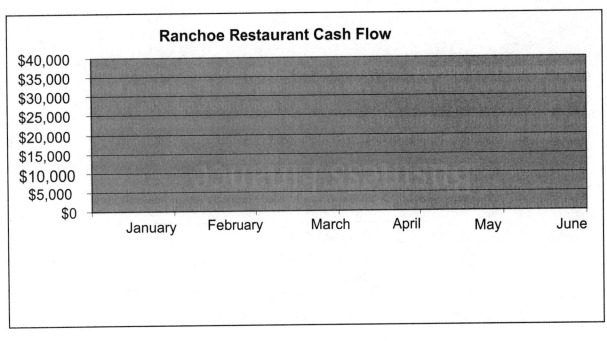

End-of-Month $____ $____ $____ $____ $____ $____
Cash Balance

36.   An entrepreneur examines his income statement for the preceding six months and identifies the following factors that relate to the financial peformance of his company:

a.   Product sales overall are stable but an older product had a sales decline of 12% from the same time period a year ago, hiding small sales increases of all other products.

b.   The cost of sales for the three-month period has declined by 5%, but the company's inventory is currently slightly lower than average due to several slow shipments from suppliers that have limited production. The lower production has not yet affected filling sales orders but could in the future if production doesn't return to normal.

c.   Operating expenses have increased by 4%. Most of the increase resulted from higher utility prices due to a severe winter and a company-wide payroll increase of 2% that went into effect at the beginning of the six-month period.

d.   Income for the period is up 4%. It is affected by the fact that a large loan had been paid off at the end of the last financial period so interest expenses are down over 50% for the six months. The owner expects that additional financing will be needed for an expansion of production in the next six months.

Based on the information from the financial analysis, write one conclusion that reflects your views of the current financial condition of the business.

Using the information, write one recommendation for the entrepreneur to strengthen the financial position of the company during the next six months.

Chapter ④ Study Guide   Maintain and Analyze Financial Records

Part 1   Yes or No

Directions   Indicate your answer to each of the following questions by placing a check mark on the line under *yes* or *no* at the right.

	Yes	**No**

1. Are the three interrelated areas that are a part of finance money and capital markets, investments, and financial management?   _____ _____

2. Is the fundamental accounting equation Owner's Equity = Assets + Liabilities?   _____ _____

3. Is the accounting cycle a series of steps performed to ensure the completeness and accuracy of accounting records and to prepare summary financial statements?   _____ _____

4. Must accountants take direction from a company's executives even if it means that some accounting principles are not followed?   _____ _____

5. Will all of the primary users of financial reports and information from a company have the same needs and uses for the information?   _____ _____

6. Is the person responsible for planning and managing a company's financial resources known as the Chief Financial Officer (CFO)?   _____ _____

7. Are the three primary financial statements of businesses the balance sheet, the income statement and the annual report?   _____ _____

8. Is cash generated in a business from operating activities, financing activities, or investing activities?   _____ _____

9. Are relationships in a company's finances studied using ratio analysis in order to understand and improve financial performance?   _____ _____

10. Is a competitor that has historically demonstrated outstanding financial performance known as a benchmark company?   _____ _____

Part 2   Completion

Directions   In the Answers column, write the word or words needed to complete each sentence.

Answers

11. The financial records for each of the specific assets, liabilities, and categories of owner's equity are known as the business' __?__.
11. _____

12. The accounting procedure that recognizes revenues and expenses when they are incurred rather than when cash is received or spent is known as __?__ accounting.
12. _____

13. Information __?__ means that information remains unchanged from its source and has not been accidentally or maliciously modified, altered, or destroyed.
13. _____

14. __?__ financing is the use of borrowed money to obtain needed assets.
14. _____

15. The ability of an organization to meet its financial obligations as they become due is known as __?__.
15. _____

16. Operating __?__ is the company's earnings before interest and taxes.
16. _____

Part 3   Matching

Directions   In the Answers column, indicate which financial record or report is best described by each statement.

A.   Balance Sheet

C.   Statement of Cash Flow

B.   Income Statement

D.   Annual Report

Answers

17.   A statement of a company's operating and financial performance issued at the end of its fiscal year.   17._____

18.   The important information contained includes the company's total assets, liabilities, and owner's equity and how each category is divided.   18._____

19.   A picture of the financial condition of the business as of a specific date.   19._____

20.   Often includes a letter from the chief executive, a narrative discussion of the year's operations, and plans for the future.   20._____

21.   Sales and the costs to generate those sales, other sources of revenue, and all operating, administrative, and other business expenses are detailed.   21._____

22.   It demonstrates the solvency of a business on a month-to-month basis or even more frequently.   22._____

Part 4   Activities

23.   You are the chief accountant for a corporation that has experienced a poor year financially. The CEO is feeling pressure from the Board of Directors and believes he may be fired. He has asked you to help him make the past year's financial performance look as good a possible by delaying reporting some major end-of-year expenses. He suggests that delaying recording the expenses for only two weeks and including them in next year's records when revenues are expected to be much higher will actually show a more balanced view of the company's ongoing financial performance. Use the space below to write a memo to the CEO expressing the actions you will take in response to his request and the reasons for your decision.

24. Accounting personnel "close the books" for an accounting period by completing each of the steps in the accounting cycle. Demonstrate your understanding of the correct order of the cycle by writing the appropriate step from the following list in the figure below. Then, in your own words, write a brief explanation of the importance of each step in the space below the figure.

Journal entries are posted in the appropriate accounts	Adjusting entries are recorded
Closing entries are completed	Transactions are recorded in journals
A trial balance of the accounts is prepared	Financial statements are prepared

The Accounting Cycle

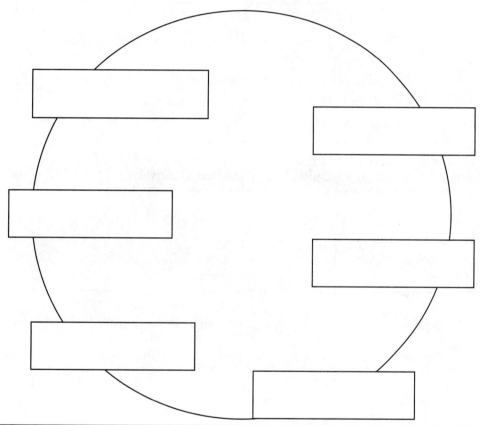

Step #	Importance
1	
2	
3	
4	
5	
6	

25. Calculate each of the following financial ratios using the data provided. Then in the space below each calculation, write a brief statement of why the ratio is important in the analysis of the financial performance of a company.

Ratio and Formula	Data	Answer
current ratio = $\dfrac{\text{current assets}}{\text{current liabilities}}$	current assets = $1,285,967 current liabilities = $856,220	
inventory turnover ratio = $\dfrac{\text{net sales}}{\text{average inventory}}$	net sales = $643,762 average inventory = $72,528	
accounts receivable turnover ratio = $\dfrac{\text{total credit sales}}{\text{accounts receivable}}$	credit sales = $2,478,119 accounts receivable = $178,020	
debt ratio = $\dfrac{\text{total debt}}{\text{total assets}}$	current assets = $256,005 current liabilities = $202,998 long-term assets = $828,040 long-term liabilities = $382,559	
return on equity ratio = $\dfrac{\text{net profit}}{\text{stockholders' equity}}$	stockholder's equity = $385,700 net profit = $26,290	

Chapter **5** Study Guide   Short-Term Financial Activities

Part 1   Unscramble

Directions   Unscramble the following vocabulary words that were discussed in Chapter 5.

Answers

1. ysraal

    1._____

2. xdceifosst (2 words)

    2._____

3. ynvtronie

    3._____

4. dbgacshuet (2 words)

    4._____

5. ataipycc

    5._____

6. mdeiretrcst (2 words)

    6._____

7. iakgnclprwioat (2 words)

    7._____

8. neesanlducuro (2 words)

    8._____

9. gsewa

    9._____

10. errtsstcunaes (2 words)

    10._____

11. atloclealr

    11._____

12. tucroternrai (2 words)

    12._____

Part 2   Matching

Directions   In the Answers column, write the word or phrase from Part 1 above that correctly matches each statement below.

Answers

13. The earnings of workers calculated on an hourly basis.

    13._____

14. The difference between current assets and current liabilities.

    14._____

15. Earnings calculated on the basis of a time period, usually weekly, bi-weekly, or monthly.

    15._____

16. A number calculated by dividing current assets by current liabilities.

    16._____

17. A specific asset used to secure a loan.

    17._____

18. Loan that has no specific collateral.

    18._____

19. The merchandise an organization plans to sell to customers.

    19._____

20. Business expenses that do not change as the level of production changes.

    20._____

21. The ability of the borrower to repay money owed.

    21._____

22. An estimate of future cash receipts and cash payments for a specified period of time.

    22._____

Part 3   Name That Pay Method

Directions   In the Answers column, match the following pay methods with their descriptions.

A.   wages

B.   salary

C.   piece rate

D.   commission

23.   Earnings determined on the basis of each unit of output.

24.   Earnings of workers calculated on an hourly basis.

25.   Compensation earned by salespeople or others as a percentage of sales.

26.   Earnings determined by the hourly rate of pay multiplied by the number of hours worked.

27.   Earnings calculated on the basis of a time period, usually weekly, bi-weekly, or monthly.

23._____

24._____

25._____

26._____

27._____

Part 4   Activities

The Cash Budget				
Cash Receipts	January	February	March	1st Quarter Total
• Cash Sales	$4,000	$6,100		$18,100
• Collection on Account	12.100	11,100	13.400	
• Other Cash Receipts		600	2,200	5,000
Total Cash Received	$18,300		$23,600	
Cash Payments	January	February	March	1st Quarter Total
• Variable Expenses	$10,200		$8,300	
• Fixed Expenses		8,600	8,600	25,800
• Other Cash Expenses	1,400	2,600		6,800
Total Cash Payments	$20,200	$18,800	$19,700	$58,700
Cash Excess (Shortage)				

28.   Calculate the missing amounts in the cash budget above.

29.   In which months did a cash shortage exist?

30.   What actions might be taken to cover the cash shortage?

31.   What concerns are associated with having a large cash excess?

32. Using the following items, calculate the amounts requested below.

    Accounts receivable: $800   Cash: $2,200
    Accounts payable: $1,500   Work in progress: $1,200
    Taxes owed: $1,250   Short-term loans: $600
    Direct materials: $700   Finished goods: $1,300

    a. What is the amount of total current assets? $_____

    b. What is the total of the current liabilities? $_____

    c. What is the amount of working capital in this situation? $_____

    d. What is the current ratio for the company? _____

33. There are three main types of inventory used by manufacturing companies. Examine the three columns below. In the first column, the three types of inventory are listed. In the middle column, descriptions of these inventory types are presented. The last column identifies several examples. Demonstrate your understanding of the types of inventory by drawing lines that connect the correct type of inventory with the description and then with examples of that type of inventory. When you have completed the connections, list two other examples for each type of inventory item.

Type of Inventory	Description	Example
Direct Materials	Products that have completed the manufacturing process and are ready to sell.	Cotton cloth
		Sweater without label
Work in Process	Parts and supplies used to create a finished product.	MP3 player
		Bottles for juice drinks
Finished Goods	Items in various stages of completion.	Radio without speaker
		Shirt

Additional examples of :

    Direct Materials   _____   _____

    Work in Process   _____   _____

    Finished Goods   _____   _____

34. Using this information, calculate the items requested below:

Selling price: $12

Variable cost per unit: $8

Total fixed costs: $57,000

a. What is the total variable cost at a production level of 10,000 units of production?

b. What is the breakeven point based on these amounts?

c. What would be the profit (or loss) at 16,000 units of production?

d. What are some examples of variable expenses for a manufacturing company?

e. What are some examples of fixed expenses?

35. Melanie Collins worked 44 hours during a recent pay period. Her pay rate is $10.60 an hour, and she earns 1.5 times the hourly rate for time worked over 40 hours. During the current pay period, she had the following deductions from her pay:

Federal income tax $56

FICA/Medicare $37

State income tax $12

Health insurance $18

Savings deposit $30

a. What is the amount of Melanie's regular wages for this pay period?

b. What is the amount of her overtime pay?

c. What is the total amount of her deductions?

d. What is Melanie's net pay?

e. What percentage of Melanie's total pay is the amount she received in her net pay?

Chapter ⑥ Study Guide   Long-Term Financial Activities

Part 1   Yes or No

Directions   Indicate your answer to each of the following questions by placing a check mark on the line under *yes* or *no* at the right.

		Yes	**No**
1.	Does a capital project refer to business spending for current operating expenses?	_____	_____
2.	Are brand names, trademarks, and patents examples of intellectual property?	_____	_____
3.	Do mutually exclusive projects involve situations in which the acceptance of one project does not allow acceptance of others?	_____	_____
4.	Does the capital budgeting process start with the forecasting of cash flows?	_____	_____
5.	Is cost of capital the interest rate used to evaluate a capital project?	_____	_____
6.	Does the cost of equity represent the required rate of return for creditors?	_____	_____
7.	Does the payback method consider the time value of money when evaluating capital projects?	_____	_____
8.	Is a major drawback of IRR that it reports a percentage rather than a dollar amount?	_____	_____
9.	Can political risks be the result of various business regulations?	_____	_____
10.	Does product diversification by a company usually increase risk?	_____	_____

Part 2   Completion

Directions   In the Answers column, write the word or words needed to complete each sentence.

		Answers
11.	Expenses that have been incurred and cannot be recovered are _____.	11._____
12.	Two or more projects that are dependent on one another are called _____.	12._____
13.	The offering of a variety of products or services is referred to as _____.	13._____
14.	A merger between two or more companies in the same type of business is called _____.	14._____
15.	Construction or purchase of a long-term asset, such as buildings and equipment, is a _____.	15._____
16.	The analysis technique used to determine how long it will take for the cash flows of a capital project to equal the original cost is called the _____.	16._____
17.	An agreement between two or more companies to share a business project is a _____.	17._____
18.	Intangible assets used by companies are referred to as _____.	18._____
19.	The value of the alternative that is given up when a decision is made is often called the _____.	19._____
20.	The discount rate at which the net present value is zero is called the _____.	20._____

Part 3 Matching

Directions In the Answers column, indicate which type of organizational strategy is best described by each statement.

A.   Centralized Organization   C.   Horizontal Integration

B.   Decentralized Organization   D.   Vertical Integration

Answers

21. A company expands through increased involvement in different stages of production and distribution.

21._____

22. Allows company decisions to be made at lower levels of the organization.

22._____

23. Decisions are made at company headquarters.

23._____

24. Managers of local stores and factory supervisors in different countries have greater authority.

24._____

25. A merger between two or more companies in the same type of business.

25._____

Part 4 Activities

26. Capital projects are viewed in five main categories, listed below. For each, describe a potential capital project that a company might select for its business operations.

Replacement project _____

_____

Cost-saving project _____

_____

New product or new market _____

_____

Government-required project _____

_____

Social benefit project _____

_____

Name _____ Class _____ Date _____

27. The capital budgeting process may be viewed in five steps, listed below. Write each step in order in the boxes provided. Then, in the lined area, describe an action a company might take related to each step.

The Capital Budgeting Process

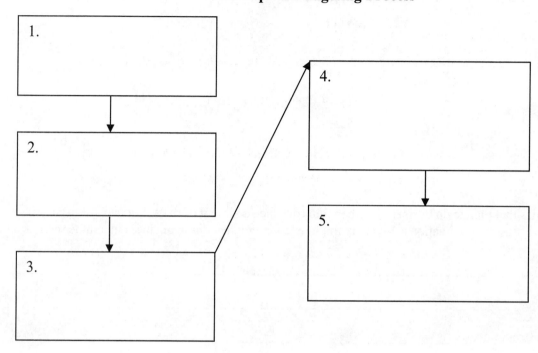

Forecast Cash Flows _____

_____

Identify Cost of Capital and Risks _____

_____

Determine Potential Projects _____

_____

Select and Implement Project _____

_____

Set Capital Spending Goals _____

_____

28. The following capital project has a cost of $26,000. The company expects the following cash flows from the project over the next few years. What is the *payback* for this project?

Year	Cash flows
1	$ 6,000
2	8,000
3	9,500
4	7,500
5	5,000

29. Companies that plan to do business in other countries face a variety of risks. For each of these risk categories, describe a situation a company might encounter when doing business in another country.

Geography _____

_____

Economic Conditions _____

_____

Social and Cultural Factors _____

_____

Political and Legal Restrictions _____

_____

As a future manager deciding where and how to do business in other countries, answer the following questions:

1. Explain why conducting business in several regions can help lower a company's business risk.

2. Describe a situation in which offering a variety of products can be a wise business strategy.

3. What concerns might occur when a company involves local ownership or employs local managers in another country to help reduce international risks?

4. Name a product (or service) and a country in which that product or service might be sold. What types of risks might a company face in that situation?

Chapter ⑦ Study Guide   Financing Business Activities

Part 1   True or False

Directions   Place a *T* for True or an *F* for False in the Answers column to show
whether each of the following statements is true or false.

Answers

1. Commercial paper is an example of a long-term financing method.

    1. _____

2. Debt financing refers to the selling of stock by a company.

    2. _____

3. Additional equity financing does not increase the risk of bankruptcy for a company.

    3. _____

4. Leasing involves renting property, equipment, or other assets.

    4. _____

5. Municipal bonds are issued by the federal government.

    5. _____

6. A mortgage bond is debt secured by a specific or other property.

    6. _____

7. Investment bankers assist companies with issuing new securities.

    7. _____

8. The coupon rate of a bond is the interest rate that changes each day in the bond market.

    8. _____

9. Bond ratings a measure of the quality and safety of a company's debt.

    9. _____

10. Common stockholders elect the board of directors of a company.

    10. _____

Part 2   Multiple Choice

Directions   In the Answers column, write the letter that represents the word, or
group of words, that correctly completes the statement.

Answers

11. Amounts owed to creditors for goods and services are called (a) a promissory note (b) accounts
    payable (c) a line of credit (d) commercial paper.

    11. _____

12. Rental of equipment, a building, land, or other assets is referred to as (a) debt financing (b)
    equity financing (c) a mortgage (d) leasing.

    12. _____

13. The federal government bond with the longest maturity is a (a) Treasury bill (b) Treasury bond
    (c) Savings bond (d) Treasury note.

    13. _____

14. The interest earned is exempt from federal and most state income taxes for a (a) U.S. savings
    bond (b) municipal bond (c) Treasury bill (d) debenture bond.

    14. _____

15. A corporate bond without collateral is (a) a municipal bond (b) a mortgage bond (c) a debenture
    bond (d) an external bond.

    15. _____

16. For a bond, 1/100 of a percentage is called (a) a basis point (b) the bond yield (c) the rate of
    return (d) a bond rating.

    16. _____

17. The location where securities are traded after they are initially offered is the (a) primary market
    (b) foreign exchange market (c) mutual funds (d) secondary market.

    17. _____

18. The increase in the value of a bond between the purchase price and the maturity value is the (a)
    capital gain (b) bond rating (c) yield to maturity (d) coupon rate.

    18. _____

Part 3   Matching

Directions   In the Answers column, indicate the financing method best described by each statement.

A.   Account payable
B.   Line of credit
C.   Promissory note

D.   Commercial paper
E.   Leasing
F.   Corporate bond

Answers

19.   An agreement that allows a company to obtain additional loans without a new loan application.   19._____

20.   Amounts owed to creditors for goods and services.   20._____

21.   A written promise to borrow money between a borrower and a lender.   21._____

22.   Unsecured, short-term debt instruments issued by corporations.   22._____

23.   A legal agreement to use property that belongs to another person.   23._____

24.   A long-term debt security used to borrow money by a company.   24._____

25.   A contract to use real estate, equipment, or other assets for a specified time, paying a monthly amount to the owner of the property   25._____

Part 4   Activities

26.   The current yield for an investment provides information on the rate of return. The current yield is calculated as follows:

$$\text{Current yield (\%)} = \frac{\text{Interest amount (\$)}}{\text{Cost of the investment}}$$

$$\text{Example: Current yield (\%)} = \frac{\$80}{\$940} = 0.085 = 8.5 \text{ percent}$$

a.   What is the current yield for a stock that costs $56 and pays a dividend of $4.76?

b.   What is the current yield for a bond costing $1,000 and paying annual interest of $93?

c.   A bond pays annual interest of $87 and has a current yield of 7 percent; what is the cost of the bond?

27.   Listed in the first column are the four categories of bond ratings. Match these categories to the descriptions in the second column.

A.   High-grade

B.   Medium-grade

C.   Speculative

D.   Default

_____   Bonds from companies that are of poor standing with extremely poor prospects for making payments to investors; company may have filed for bankruptcy.

_____   Bonds judged to be somewhat uncertain and a fairly high risk.

_____   These ratings are assigned companies judged to be of high quality by all standards; almost no chance of default.

_____   Bonds from companies that have many favorable factors with very little chance of default.

28. When companies issue stock for the first time or issue additional shares, four steps are involved:

    Obtain needed approval   Set price through underwriting process

    Consult with investment banker   Notify the public of the issue

Place these steps in the correct order and describe the activities involved with each step.

Step. 1 _____   _____

                                                _____

Step. 2 _____   _____

                                                _____

Step. 3 _____   _____

                                                _____

Step. 4 _____   _____

                                                _____

29. Mutual funds are used by investors to achieve various financial goals. Listed here are some of the main types of mutual funds:

    a.   Aggressive growth stock fund
    b.   Income fund
    c.   International fund
    d.   Sector fund
    e.   Bond fund
    f.   Balanced fund

For the following investment situations, select one of the funds that a person might use to achieve the investment goal and explain why that fund is a good choice.

Investment Situation	Type of Mutual Fund	Explanation
1. An investor who desires the safety of debt securities.		
2. A retired person who wants income from investments.		
3. A person who wants to invest in a variety of companies in the automotive industry.		
4. A person who attempts to earn money based on the success of companies in various countries.		
5. Someone who wishes to earn based on investments in both stocks and bonds.		

30. Analyze the following daily stock report. Answer the questions below.

STOCK MARKET QUOTATIONS

1	2	3	4	5	6	7	8	9	10	11	12
52-Week					Yld.		Vol.				Net
Hi	Lo	Stock	Sym.	Div.	%	PE	100s	Hi	Lo	Close	Chg.
74.93	56.72	Deere	DE	1.12	1.6	15	21823	70.14	67.38	68.01	−0.42
95.64	64.84	FedExCp	FDX	0.28	0.3	27	14555	94.54	91.78	93.74	+1.22
45	35	Kellogg	K	1.01	2.3	21	6791	44.82	43.67	44.74	−0.24
20.50	15.94	Mattel	MAT	0.40	2.1	16	21682	19.23	17.77	18.80	−0.15
42.95	31.25	Reebok	RBK	0.30	0.8	14	4501	40.47	37.82	39.22	+0.12

a. What was the highest price paid for a share of Kellogg stock over the past year?

b. What was the closing price of Mattel on the previous trading day?

c. How many shares of FedEx stock were sold on this trading day?

d. If a person owned 500 shares of Deere, how much would be received in dividends?

e. Based on the closing price for Reebok, if the company paid an annual dividend of $2.28, what would be the yield?

f. What company and economic factors could cause the value of FedEx stock to continue to increase?

31. On a daily basis, bond prices change in value. Here is a table that summarizes possible changes for the bond of a company. Use this information to answer the questions below.

SITUATION	BOND SOLD AT	MARKET VALUE	REPORTED AT	INTEREST PAYMENT	CURRENT YIELD
Bond issued	par	$1,000	100	$100	10 % ($100 ÷ $1,000)
Higher interest rates	discount	$ 800	(a)	(b)	(c)
Lower interest rates	premium	(d)	120	$100	8.33 % ($100 ÷ $1,200)

a. What would a bond with a market value of $800 be reported at on the bond market reports?

b. What would be the interest payment for this bond?

c. What would be the yield for this bond?

d. When a bond is reported at 120, what is the market value?

e. Why does the interest payment ($100) on this bond stay the same?

f. What types of risks might occur that would reduce the value of a company's bond?

Chapter ⑧ Study Guide Financial Institutions and Banking Services

Part 1 Yes or No

Directions Indicate your answer to each of the following questions by placing a check mark on the line under *yes* or *no* at the right.

		Yes	**No**

1. Has the Federal Reserve System issued federal banknotes since 1776? _____ _____

2. Is the regulation of the money supply one of the activities of the Federal Reserve System? _____ _____

3. Does decreasing the reserve requirement increase the money supply in the economy? _____ _____

4. Does the Comptroller of the Currency protect the bank deposits of consumers? _____ _____

5. Does commercial banking refer to services provided to businesses? _____ _____

6. Is a life insurance company an example of a depository financial intermediary? _____ _____

7. Does a *financial supermarket* refer to a bank branch in a food store? _____ _____

8. Is direct deposit used by companies to pay workers? _____ _____

9. Are payments made with a debit card subtracted from your checking account? _____ _____

10. Do banks offer mortgages as well as business loans? _____ _____

11. Do bridge loans allow a business to obtain additional funds, up to a certain amount, without a new loan application? _____ _____

12. Does a development bank provide financing for economic development to countries in a geographic region? _____ _____

Part 2 Completion

Directions In the Answers column, write the word or words needed to complete each sentence.

Answers

13. A secured postal box used to receive customer payments is a _____. 13._____

14. The _____ is the rate the Federal Reserve System charges on loans to member banks. 14._____

15. The percentage of funds that a bank is required to hold on deposit is the _____. 15._____

16. The _____ was created with the main function of providing economic assistance to less-developed countries. 16._____

17. _____ lending refers to loans to businesses. 17._____

18. The process of buying and selling government securities is called _____. 18._____

19. The legal agreement for one party to control property for the benefit of another is a _____. 19._____

20. A _____ is a place banks offer where customers can store valuables. 20._____

Part 3 Matching

Directions In the Answers column, indicate which financial institution is best described by each statement.

A. Commercial bank
B. Savings and loan association
C. Credit union

D. Life insurance company
E. Investment company
F. Mortgage company

Answers

21. Provides financial protection for the dependents of people who purchase the policies.

21._____

22. Has traditionally specialized in savings accounts and home mortgages.

22._____

23. Usually offers the widest range of services to both individuals and business customers.

23._____

24. Has the primary function of lending money for home buying.

24._____

25. A nonprofit financial organization.

25._____

26. Its main focus is on pooling funds from many people to select investments with growth opportunities.

26._____

27. Offers services to meet the needs of their owner-customers.

27._____

Part 4 Activities

28. The following is a map of the Federal Reserve Banks and the branch banks of the Federal Reserve System. Use this map to answer the questions below.

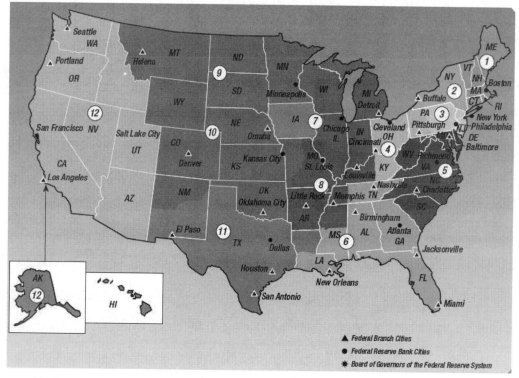

a. Circle the city of the Federal Reserve Bank for the district in which you live.

b. What is the district number in which Utah is located?

c. A bank doing business in Detroit would make use of the services in which Federal Reserve Bank city?

d. What is the district number for Mississippi?

29. Three major federal government agencies regulate banking activities. Match the agencies with the descriptions listed.

A. Federal Reserve System

B. Federal Deposit Insurance Corporation

C. Comptroller of the Currency

_____ 1. Evaluates a bank management's ability to identify and control risk.

_____ 2. Examines loans and investments of national banks with regard to liquidity, risk, and banking laws.

_____ 3. Buys and sells government securities to influence money supply.

_____ 4. Provides a federal government guarantee of deposits.

_____ 5. Sets interest rates that can affect borrowing in the economy.

30. The Federal Reserve System has three main tools that are used to affect the money supply in the economy. For each one, describe what action would be taken to (a) increase and (b) decrease the money supply.

MONETARY POLICY	(a) INCREASE MONEY SUPPLY	(b) DECREASE MONEY SUPPLY
Setting reserve requirements		
Changing the discount rate		
Buying and selling government securities		

31. Businesses and consumers use five main types of financial services. For each category, describe how consumers and businesses would use these financial services.

Type of financial service	Consumer use	Business use
Electronic Banking		
Savings Services		
Payment Services		
Lending Services		
Other Services		

32. Various international banking and financial agencies exist to assist companies and countries. Draw lines to connect each agency to the description of that agency.

Global Banking Agency	Description
World Bank	Promotes economic cooperation by maintaining an orderly system of international trade and exchange rates.
International Monetary Fund	An organization of countries created to provide financing for economic development to countries in a geographic region.
Organization for Economic Cooperation and Development	Has the main function of providing economic assistance to less-developed countries to build communications networks, transportation systems, and utility plants.
Regional development banks	Industrialized nations committed to democratic government and the market economy, to expand free trade and encourage economic development.

33. Several high-cost financial service companies exist. These organizations include pawnshops, check-cashing outlets, payday loan companies, and rent-to-own centers. Select two of these businesses and (a) explain dangers of using this financial service, and (b) describe actions that might be taken to avoid these high-cost financial services.

      (a) Dangers of using this service   (b) Actions that might be taken to avoid

Chapter ⑨ Study Guide   Customer Credit

Part 1   True or False

Directions   Place a *T* for True or an *F* for False in the Answers column to show whether each of the following statements is true or false.

1. The goal of all companies in completing the production-sales cycle is to maximize revenues.   1._____

2. Deciding to extend credit to customers or use credit when making purchases should be viewed primarily as a financial decision.   2._____

3. Legally, a company cannot evaluate individuals and businesses to determine if they are a good credit risk since that would be evidence of discrimination.   3._____

4. The largest expense for a company when using a contracted credit plan is a discount from the sale price that the business must pay to the credit card company on each transaction.   4._____

5. It is a wise financial decision for businesses to make credit generally available for all products any time they are offered for sale.   5._____

6. It is a common practice when offering business credit to encourage early payment to offer the buyer a price discount if payment is made quickly.   6._____

7. The two most important factors when determining an individual's credit score are the credit payment history and the number and amount of credit accounts.   7._____

8. Factoring involves selling accounts receivable at a discount to a private company that then becomes responsible for collecting the accounts.   8._____

9. A credit account that has not been paid by the due date is known as a charge-off.   9._____

10. The final step in the collections process should always be to take legal action.   10._____

Part 2   Multiple Choice

Directions   In the Answers column, write the letter that represents the word, or group of words, that correctly completes the statement.

11. An agreement in which a borrower receives something of value in exchange for a promise to repay the lender at a later date is (a) financing (b) a sales contract (c) credit (d) collateral.   11._____

12. U.S. consumers used credit cards to finance short-term purchases of over $__?__ in a recent year. (a) $1 million (b) $100 million (c) $2 trillion (d) $200 trillion.   12._____

13. Criteria businesses should use to decide when to offer credit include all of the following *except* offering credit (a) to specific categories of customers (b) for specific types of products (c) during specific times of the year (d) only in specific areas of the country.   13._____

14. Which of the following is *not* one of the three companies that are the primary sources of consumer credit information in the U.S.? (a) Dun & Bradstreet (b) Experian (c) TransUnion (d) Equifax.   14._____

15. If interest is compound rather than simple, the amount of interest paid over the period of the loan will be (a) higher (b) lower (c) the same amount (d) higher for the first year, then lower.   15._____

16. Categorizing all accounts receivable by the length of time they remain unpaid is known as (a) auditing (b) aging (c) organizing (d) factoring.   16._____

Part 3   Matching

Directions   In the Answers column, indicate which federal credit law is directed at the action described by each statement.

A.	Truth-in-Lending Act	E.	Fair Debt Collection Practices Act
B.	Equal Credit Opportunity Act	F.	Right to Financial Privacy Act
C.	Fair Credit Reporting Act	G.	Financial Modernization Act
D.	Fair Credit Billing Act		

Answers

17. Imposes requirements on financial institutions for communicating with customers prior to release of personal information.

17. _____

18. Developed to increase the accuracy and privacy of information collected by credit reporting companies.

18. _____

19. Includes the Safeguards Rule, which requires all financial institutions to maintain safeguards to protect customer information.

19. _____

20. Designed to promote the informed use of credit and encourage consumers to compare the cost of cash versus credit as well as to shop for the least expensive credit.

20. _____

21. Prohibits discrimination against credit applicants because of age, sex, marital status, religion, race, color, national origin, or receipt of public assistance.

21. _____

22. Prohibits unfair, deceptive, or abusive practices when dealing with people who have overdue accounts.

22. _____

23. Deals with mistakes in credit bills sent to consumers.

23, _____

Part 4   Activities

24. Protecting personal information through effective online security measures has become one of the most important requirements for everyone using any type of online communications or business services. Preparing, remembering, and using specific security procedures will greatly reduce your chances of having your personal identity stolen, financial accounts compromised, or computer software and files hacked and damaged. The chart below presents several specific situations where your online security is at risk. For each situation, write one specific action you can take that will reduce the online threats you face. When you have finished, make a personal commitment to take each step regularly to increase your personal security.

To deal with the security issue related to:	I will take the following action:
Hackers, viruses, and spyware	
Making online purchases	
Stealing account passwords	
Use of personal information	
Stolen credit card numbers or account information	

25. Your creditworthiness is one of your most valuable personal resources. With a strong credit rating, you will be able to access financing when you need it and usually with much better credit terms than will be offered to someone with a poor credit history. Even if you don't have any immediate needs for personal credit, you can begin now to build your creditworthiness. Businesses use the 4 C's of credit to evaluate credit eligibility. Each of the 4 C's is identified in the space below. Conduct a personal evaluation of your current strengths for each of the C's and list them in the appropriate area. Then list steps you can take or things you can do to improve your qualifications in each area and build your creditworthiness.

MY 4 C'S OF CREDIT

CHARACTER	CAPACITY
My Current Strengths	**My Current Strengths**
Steps to Improve My Creditworthiness	**Steps to Improve My Creditworthiness**

COLLATERAL	CONDITIONS
My Current Strengths	**My Current Strengths**
Steps to Improve My Creditworthiness	**Steps to Improve My Creditworthiness**

26. The following statements describe the steps in a company's credit collections procedures. Complete each statement by filling in the blanks to spell the missing words correctly.

STEPS IN AN EFFECTIVE COLLECTIONS PROCEDURE

1. Carefully _ _ _ _ _ _   _ _ _ _ _ _ applications.

2. Maintain _ _ _ _ _ _ _ _ and _ _ - _ _ - _ _ _ _ account information.

3. Ensure _ _ _ _ _ _ and accurate _ _ _ _ _ _ _ _ _.

4. _ _ _ _ _ _ _ accounts receivable.

5. Take immediate _ _ _ _ _ _ following established _ _ _ _ _ _ _ _ _ _.

6. Use _ _ _ _ _ _ _ _ _ – _ _ _ _ _ _ _ _ but effective collection strategies.

7. _ _ _ _ _ _ _ _ collections before it is too late.

8. Establish final collection and _ _ _ _ _ _ _ – _ _ _ standards.

27. Partine Partners has a credit policy of net 30 days. The current status of credit accounts is shown in the following table. Complete the Aging of Accounts analysis for the company by calculating the total and percentage of total for each account and each aging category.

			Partine Partners Age of Accounts Receivable				
Account	0–30 days	31–60 days	61–90 days	91–120 days	over 120 days	Account Total	% of Total Receivables
J. Ahrens	$120	$240		$60			
L. Coleell				$1,080	$690		
M. Firstall	$458			$65			
P. Jacobs	$220	$368	$190				
B. Monez					$850		
K. Pierelli		$900					
J.Thomas	$18	$568	$25		$110		
A. Vartok	$2,451						
Age Total							
% of Total Receivables							

Analyze the Aging of Accounts data and answer the following questions:

a. Which individual account presents the greatest problem for Partine Partners?

b. Which individual account appears to be the best credit customer?

c. Do you believe Partine Partners has an effective credit collection policy and procedures or not? Why?

d. What advice would you give Partine Partners to improve their accounts receivable?

Chapter ⬤10 Study Guide Business Insurance

Part 1   Unscramble

Directions   Unscramble the following vocabulary words that were discussed in Chapter 10.

Answers

1. coomicenskir (2 words)   1._____
2. gansimaemkrnet (2 words)   2._____
3. naruinsce   3._____
4. yioplc   4._____
5. sunirde   5._____
6. rerunis   6._____
7. lerip   7._____
8. holycilopred   8._____
9. inetebrsitsnualer (2 words) 9._____
10. ddeeblitcu   10._____
11. ybreaniecfi   11._____
12. lavciiblliiity (2 words)   12._____

Part 2   Matching

Directions   In the Answers column, write the word or phrase from Part 1 above that correctly matches each definition below.

Answers

13. A legal contract through which insurance is implemented.   13._____

14. The individual or organization to whom the policy is issued.   14._____

15. Has a potential financial impact.   15._____

16. A person or organization designated to receive the proceeds of the insurance 16._____
    policy.

17. The cause of a loss.   17._____

18. A contract providing financial protection against a specified loss.   18._____

19. An identified amount of a loss that must be paid by the insured before the   19._____
    insurer pays.

20. The insured will suffer a financial loss if the insured event occurs.   20._____

21. The process of systematically identifying potential risks and making plans to   21._____
    reduce the impact of the risk on individuals and companies.

22. The company that assumes the risk and agrees to pay losses covered by the   22._____
    policy.

Part 3 Yes or No

Directions Indicate your answer to each of the following questions by placing a
check mark on the line under *yes* or *no* at the right.

		Yes	**No**
23.	Each day as you go through your typical routine do you face uncertainty and risk?	____	____
24.	Are people willing to take risks because of the opportunities presented?	____	____
25.	Can some risks actually be avoided?	____	____
26.	Might a company choose to assume a risk if it is relatively small or unlikely to occur?	____	____
27.	With insurance, does the risk facing any one business increase in order to reduce the risk for all of the businesses that are insured?	____	____
28.	Insurance is not a legally enforceable contract, so if the insurance company chooses not to pay is there little the policyholder can do?	____	____
29.	Is it possible to accurately estimate the amount of losses that an insurance company must pay?	____	____
30.	In order for a risk to be insurable, must the losses from the perils be controllable and certain to occur?	____	____
31.	Does an adjuster work for an insurance company and determine the extent of a loss and the liability of the insurer?	____	____

Part 4 Activities

32. Both individuals and businesses face risks. The four methods of dealing with risks are

> AV = avoid the risk   TR = transfer the risk
> IN = insure the risk   AS = assume the risk

Read each of the statements below and identify the method the business used to deal with the risk
described. Write the letters for the method you selected in the Answers column.

Answers

a.   Safety research shows a new children's toy may break when used incorrectly. The
company decides not to market the product until further product development can be
completed.

a. _____

b.   A construction company hires smaller firms to complete some of the work on the homes
it builds. It purchases a surety bond to assure customers that work will be completed as
specified.

b. _____

c.   Due the inability of a new interior design business to predict the amount of credit sales
and the cost of collections, it decides to contract with a credit specialist to design and
administer a credit system.

c. _____

d.   An irrigation company approaches the owner of a 1,000-acre vegetable farm in South
Florida to sell a misting system that protects crops against freezing temperatures. Since on
average the temperature in the area falls below freezing only once in 20 years, the farmer
decides not to purchase the equipment.

e. _____

e.   An airline is concerned that fuel prices will double in the next year, so it contracts for a
year's supply of fuel on the futures market at 15 percent above the current price.

f. _____

33. An important responsibility of a business owner or risk manager is to identify insurance companies that are able to insure the types of risks faced by the company. The Insurance Department or Office of the Insurance Commissioner of each state maintains a list of insurance companies that are approved to sell insurance in the state (*http://www.naic.org/state_web_map.htm*). Use the Internet to identify a company from which a business in your state could purchase each type of insurance listed in the table below. Then gather the required information about the company selected. Finally, answer the questions below the table about how you would make choices of insurance companies if you were a business owner.

Type of Insurance	Insurance Company Name and Headquarters Address	Type of Ownership (stock or mutual company)	Is insurance sold through company agents or independent agents?
Property Insurance			
Vehicle Insurance			
Health Insurance			
Life Insurance			
Worker's Compensation Insurance			
Liability Insurance			

a. Is it preferable to buy all of a business' insurance through one company or to use several companies?

b. What criteria would you use to select the business' primary insurance company?

c. Would you prefer to purchase insurance through a company agent or an independent agent?

34. The National Association of Insurance Commissioners reports on the total amount of insurance in force each year for various types of commercial insurance. The total premiums paid in 2000 and 2005 for major types of commercial insurance are compared in the following table. Using the information, complete the table by calculating the dollar increase in premiums and the percentage of increase for each type of insurance between 2000 and 2005.

Type of Insurance	2000 Premiums ($000)	2005 Premiums ($000)	Dollar Increase 2000–2005	Percentage Increase 2000–2005
Worker's Compensation	$26,185,928	$39,920,684		
Commercial Automobile	13,734,120	19,831,766		
Commercial Multiple Peril	20,072,151	29,693,913		
General Liability	20,127,095	43,151,462		
Fire Insurance	4,740,558	8,030,308		
Inland Marine	6,577,227	8,256,077		
Surety Bonds	3,362,627	3,828,367		
Fidelity Bonds	815,007	1,219,587		
Burglary and Theft	116,885	120,659		
Reinsurance	24,853,859	25,330,697		

35. According to 2006 Fortune 500 rankings, the largest U.S. stock insurance company was American International Group (AIG). The largest U.S. mutual insurance company that year was State Farm Insurance Companies. The 2005 financial performance of each company was:

Company	Revenues (mil.)	Profits (mil.)	Assets (mil.)	Owner's Equity (mil.)
AIG	108,905	10,477	853,370	86,317
State Farm	59,224	3,242	159,669	50,229

a. For each company, calculate:

	AIG	State Farm
Return on Revenue (profit ÷ revenue)	_____	_____
Return on Assets (profit ÷ assets)	_____	_____
Return on Owner's Equity (profit ÷ OE)	_____	_____

b. Analyze the companies' financial performance using the ratios you have calculated.

c. Why would an person invest in State Farm rather than AIG?

40

Chapter ⬤11 Study Guide   Technology and Financial Management

Part 1   Yes or No

Directions   Indicate your answer to each of the following questions by placing a check mark on the line under *yes* or *no* at the right.

	Yes	**No**

1. Even though much of the information in the financial industry has moved from paper-based to electronic, has the speed at which information flows increased?

2. Is it true that, in past years, an important reason why businesses could not replace some paper documents with electronic alternatives were laws that restricted their use?

3. Does the U.S. currently have the largest number of Internet users of any country in the world?

4. Is the ability to collaborate in the analysis of financial information and decision-making an important requirement of information systems?

5. While many large multinational businesses have made the change, do most businesses not feel they currently have to increase the use of technology?

6. Typically when a business introduces new technology, can it immediately replace older products and processes?

7. Is an opportunity cost the direct cost of purchasing and implementing any new technology?

8. Has the insurance industry been one of the last categories of financial services to accept and implement consumer-oriented technology?

9. Has new technology almost eliminated the security issues facing the financial industry?

10. Are financial services companies legally required to give consumers privacy notices that explain the institutions' information-sharing practices?

Part 2   Completion

Directions   In the Answers column, write the word or words needed to complete each sentence.

Answers

11. With _____-___ planning, alternatives for financial decisions are considered by applying assumptions to the financial data in an electronic spreadsheet.

11._____

12. Data _____ means that information has not been altered or destroyed in an unauthorized manner.

12._____

13. Information _____ is the right of an individual to be secure from unauthorized disclosure of information.

13._____

14. _____ _____ occurs when someone uses your personal information without your permission to commit fraud or other crimes.

14._____

15. Account _____ is obtaining access to another person's financial accounts through fraud and then stealing the funds.

15._____

16. _____ attacks a legitimate business' server to redirect traffic from its web site to another web site.

16._____

Part 3 Matching

Directions   In the Answers column, indicate which stage of the Adoption Curve is best described by each statement.

A.   Innovators

B.   Early adopters

C.   Early majority

D.   Late majority

E.   Laggards

Answers

17. They want to be seen by others as accepting and using innovation. They respect and follow the   17._____
lead of others but are more value conscious and not as willing to take a risk.

18. These consumers are very resistant to change and very conservative in their purchase behavior.   18._____

19. They are viewed as opinion leaders and are quick to adopt an innovation after they have seen its   19._____
use and value.

20. The small group of consumers who are willing to pay more and put up with early problems in   20._____
order to be the first to obtain a new product. The group is made up of risk takers who want to
be the first to try something new.

21. This group is cautious and conservative and want clear evidence of the effectiveness of an   21._____
innovation.

Part 4 Activities

22. Use the following spreadsheet to complete a "what-if" analysis for a company's cash budget. Calculate
the effect of a 10% increase in all cash inflows and outflows. Then calculate the effect of a 5% decrease
on the inflows and outflows. Note: The beginning cash balance should remain the same for each
analysis.

Cash Budget Analysis

	Beginning budget	10% increase	5% decrease
Beginning Cash Balance	38,500.00	38,500.00	38,500.00
Estimated Cash Inflows			
Cash Sales	22,950.00		
Collections on Accts. Rec.	11,080.00		
New Bank Loans	5,000.00		
Total Cash Inflows	39,030.00		
Estimated Cash Outflows			
Cash Payments	31,500.00		
Payments on Accounts	4,210.00		
Lease Payments	2,950.00		
Bank Loan Payments	8,200.00		
Tax Prepayments	950.00		
Total Cash Outflows	47,810.00		
Estimated Ending Cash Balance	29,720.00		

23. Technology is changing at an ever-increasing rate and having a profound impact on businesses and consumers' lives. The finance industry is affected by technology as much as or more than other industries. Use the Internet to identify a new technology application that is being used by businesses in each of the three major parts of the finance industry—banking, investing, and insurance. Study the technology and, in the spaces below, write a short description of the technology and how the technology is used. Then describe important benefits of the technology to businesses and their customers.

Technology and Banking

Description and Use
Benefits to Businesses and Customers

Technology and Investing

Description and Use
Benefits to Businesses and Customers

Technology and Insurance

Description and Use
Benefits to Businesses and Customers

24. Identity theft is a major problem facing businesses and consumers. Yet may consumers who use the Internet regularly for personal communications, obtaining information, and completing online transactions with businesses are not aware of the problem or what they should do to protect their personal information and reduce the chances of identity theft. Develop and record a 30-second consumer information announcement designed to increase awareness about identity theft prevention. In the space below, draw an illustration that can be used with your announcement to reinforce the message. The illustration can be transferred to a large poster or other medium.

25. Consumers' preferred payment methods for in-store and online purchases are shown in the following table. A business had $289,500 of sales in one month. Fifty-eight percent of the sales were made by customers in the store and the remainder resulted from online purchases. Use the percentages to calculate the amount of receipts for each method of payment and then the total receipts and percentage of that total accounted for by each payment method, combining in-store and online purchases.

Payment Method	In-store Purchase		Online Purchase		Total Receipts	Percent of Total
	Percent	Receipts	Percent	Receipts		
Cash	33%		0%			
Check/money order	14%		8%			
Credit card	19%		55%			
Debit card	23%		25%			
Other	11%		12%			

Chapter **12** Study Guide   International Finance

Part 1   True or False

Directions   Place a *T* for True or an *F* for False in the Answers column to show whether each of the following statements is true or false.

Answers

1. Quotas encourage free trade among countries.

2. A common market often results in higher tariffs.

3. When a country exports more than it imports, a trade surplus exists.

4. Tourists visiting a country will improve the country's balance of payments.

5. Industrialized countries have an economy with a strong emphasis on agriculture or mining.

6. Lower inflation will usually result in a stronger foreign exchange rate.

7. Stock exchanges exist in only a few countries around the world.

8. Futures contracts are used to buy and sell various commodities, such corn, wheat, and gold.

9. Cash in advance is considered the lowest risk payment method when doing business in other countries.

10. The Export-Import Bank provides investment insurance to U.S. companies that establish operations in developing countries.

1._____
2._____
3._____
4._____
5._____
6._____
7._____
8._____
9._____
10._____

Part 2   Multiple Choice

Directions   In the Answers column, write the letter that represents the word, or group of words, that correctly completes the statement.

Answers

11. When a country can produce a good or service at a lower cost than other countries, it is referred to as (a) a trade barrier (b) an absolute advantage (c) a comparative advantage (d) exporting.

12. An action that would encourage trade with a country is (a) a tariff (b) an embargo (c) a free-trade zone (d) a quota.

13. A country's balance of trade would improve when (a) imports decline (b) imports increase (c) exports increase (d) higher inflation occurs.

14. Transportation, communication, and utility systems of a nation are referred to as (a) trade barriers (b) infrastructure (c) tariffs (d) imports.

15. The value of a country's currency will decline due to (a) improved political stability (b) a favorable balance of trade (c) an unfavorable balance of trade (d) lower inflation.

16. A group of stocks that are used to reflect the overall progress of many stocks is called (a) a global stock index (b) an American Depository Receipt (c) a mutual fund (d) a futures contract.

17. A written order by an exporter to an importer to make payment, usually through a third party, is (a) a commercial invoice (b) a letter of credit (c) proof of insurance (d) a bill of exchange.

18. Protection from loss when selling on account is available through the (a) Foreign Credit Insurance Association (b) World Bank (c) Export-Import Bank (d) Overseas Private Investment Corporation.

11._____
12._____
13._____
14._____
15._____
16._____
17._____
18._____

Part 3 Matching

Directions In the Answers column, indicate which international trade organization or agreement is best described by each statement.

A. Free-Trade Zone

B. Free-Trade Agreement

C. Common Market

D. Regional Trade Organization

Answers

19. When countries unite to promote economic development and trade in a geographic area.

19._____

20. An arrangement in which member countries agree to eliminate duties and trade barriers on products traded among them.

20._____

21. An area, usually around a seaport or airport, where products can be imported duty-free and then stored, assembled, and/or used in manufacturing.

21._____

22. NAFTA and CAFTA are examples of this trade arrangement.

22._____

23. Also called an *economic community*, member countries eliminate tariffs and other trade barriers to allow companies to invest freely and to allow workers to move freely across borders.

23._____

Part 4 Activities

24. A country may obtain an absolute or a comparative advantage as a result of natural resources, labor skills, or technology. Give an example of each that might occur in one or more countries.

Absolute Advantage	Comparative Advantage
_____	_____
_____	_____
_____	_____
_____	_____

25. Companies can face a variety of trade barriers when doing business around the world. Listed here are three types of formal trade barriers. Describe an example of each. Then, describe an informal trade barrier, which can result from cultural differences.

Quota   Tariff   Embargo

Informal trade barrier:

26. The value of a country's currency is influenced by three main factors. For each of the following situations, tell if the country's currency would INCREASE or DECREASE in value.

Situation	Currency Value Increase or Decrease?
Expanded exports by the country's businesses	
Improved political stability	
Higher inflation in the country	
Lower interest rates in the country	
Imports into the country grow faster than exports	

27. The level of economic development is affected by three main factors. Briefly describe each for the different categories of economies.

Economic development factor	Industrialized countries .	Less-developed countries	Developing countries
Literacy level			
Technology			
Agricultural dependency			

28. Several payment methods and documents are used in international financial transactions. Draw lines to connect each one to its description.

International Payment Methods and Documents	Description
Letter of credit	A guarantee to pay a set amount by a certain date; this document is signed by buyers to confirm their intention to make payment.
Promissory note	Prepared by the exporter, this describes the merchandise and the terms of the sale.
Bill of exchange	a financial document issued by a bank for an importer in which the bank guarantees payment.
Commercial invoice	Often required in import-export transactions, this document explains the amount of coverage for potential loss from fire, theft, water, or other damage that may occur during shipment.
Proof of insurance	A written order by an exporter to an importer to make payment, usually through a third party; includes instructions with the amount, due date, and payment location, such as a bank.

29. A company plans to do business in several other countries. Describe how this organization might use the services of the agencies listed here to assist them with financing, financial transactions, and reducing foreign trade risk.

Financial agency	**Description of how services might be used**
Export-Import Bank	
Overseas Private Investment Corporation	
Foreign Credit Insurance Association	

30. Several types of financial markets exist around the world. Listed here are four commonly active in various business settings:

international stock exchange   global bond market

foreign exchange market   futures market

Select one of these markets and conduct research for current news about this financial market. Use library resources or conduct an Internet search to obtain the information requested here.

a. Source of the information (title of article or web site, date, pages or web address).

b. Summarize the key ideas of the article or information. Be specific. Give facts and other data.

c. Describe how this information might affect the economy of a country or business activities around the world.

d. What additional questions do you have after reading this information?